Jungle Life

by Janine Scott

Content and Reading Adviser: Joan Stewart
Educational Consultant/Literacy Specialist
New York Public Schools

Compass Point Books ✦ Minneapolis, Minnesota

Compass Point Books
3109 West 50th Street, #115
Minneapolis, MN 55410

Visit Compass Point Books on the Internet at *www.compasspointbooks.com*
or e-mail your request to *custserv@compasspointbooks.com*

Photographs ©:
DigitalVision, cover; Corel, 5; Corbis, 6; Corel, 7; DigitalVision, 8, 9; PhotoDisc, 10; Corel, 11, 12;
PhotoDisc, 13, 14, 15; Visuals Unlimited/K. B. Sandved, 16; Visuals Unlimited/Joe McDonald, 17;
PhotoDisc, 18; DigitalVision, 19; Two Coyote Studios/Mary Walker Foley, 20, 21.

Project Manager: Rebecca Weber McEwen
Editor: Jennifer Waters
Photo Researcher: Jennifer Waters
Photo Selectors: Rebecca Weber McEwen and Jennifer Waters
Designer: Mary Walker Foley

Library of Congress Cataloging-in-Publication Data

Scott, Janine.
  Jungle life / by Janine Scott.
    p. cm. -- (Spyglass books)
Includes bibliographical references (p.   ).
  ISBN 978-0-7565-0235-5 (hardcover)
  ISBN 978-0-7565-1042-8 (paperback)
  1. Jungles--Juvenile literature. [1. Rain forests.] I. Title. II.
Series.
  QH86 .S37 2002
  591.734--dc21

                    2001007335

Contents

Wet and Wild

When you think of
a rain forest, you may think
of a hot, steamy jungle.
This is a *tropical* rain forest,
which is warm and wet all
year long.

Temperate rain forests
also get a lot of rain,
but they are cooler.

Did You Know?
It can rain
more than
100 inches
(254 centimeters)
a year in
a rain forest.

A rain forest has several different layers: the forest floor, the **understory**, and the *canopy*.

Different animals and plants live in the different layers. Mudskippers live in muddy puddles. A spider monkey is at home in the treetops.

Mudskipper

Spider monkey

The Forest Floor

The forest floor is the bottom layer. There is not much sunlight, so few plants grow on the floor.

Beetles, spiders, and other insects live in the fallen leaves.

Spider web

Did You Know?
Frogs and lizards hunt insects on the forest floor.

The floor is dark and shady.

The Understory

The understory is the middle layer. In the understory, vines creep up tree trunks to reach the sunlight.

Sloths, snakes, bats, and owls usually live in the understory.

Snake

A sloth hangs from a strong branch.

Life at the Top

The top layer is the canopy. Way up in the canopy there are lots of leaves and fruit to eat.

Many birds and other animals can live in this layer.

Macaw

Did You Know?
Some animals that live in the canopy never come down to the ground!

Bat

Food

Butterflies, bees, and some bats fly from flower to flower to eat nectar.
Some rain forest animals eat other animals to *survive*.

Chimpanzees eat the fruit, nuts, and seeds that grow in the rain forest.

Butterfly

Bee

Chimpanzee

15

Water

Even when it is not raining, the rain forest is a wet place to live.

The rain fills the streams and rivers of the rain forest. Many animals live in the water or close to its edge.

Piranhas

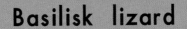

Basilisk lizard

Did You Know?
The basilisk lizard
is so small and fast,
it can run on water!

Through the Trees

The forest cats, including
jaguars, ocelots, and leopards,
are the most famous of
the jungle creatures.
They are good climbers.
They can move through
the trees in complete silence.

Monkeys have
special feet
that help them
safely run up
and down
tree branches.

Jaguar

Make a Rain Forest

You will need:
- a plant
- water
- tape
- a clear plastic bag

1. Water a plant.

2. Cover with a bag.

3. Tape the bag around the pot. Leave overnight.

4. In the morning, the warm, moist air inside the bag will be like the air in a rain forest.

5. Take the bag off the plant.

Glossary

canopy—the layer of a rain forest where the tops of the trees touch to form a "roof" on the forest

survive—to stay safe and alive

temperate—describes a rain forest that has a cooler climate

tropical—describes a rain forest that is warm and wet the entire year. Tropical rain forests are near the equator.

understory—the layer of trees beneath the canopy

Learn More

Books

Baker, Alan. *The Rain Forest.* New York: Peter Bedrick Books, 1999.

Darling, Kathy. *Rain Forest Babies.* Photographs by Tara Darling. New York: Walker and Company, 1996.

Hess, Paul. *Rainforest Animals.* New York: De Agostini Editions, 1996.

On the Web

For more information on this topic, use FactHound.

1. Go to *www.facthound.com*
2. Type in this book ID: 0756502357
3. Click on the *Fetch It* button.

FactHound will find the best Web sites for you.

Index

GR: H
Word Count: 268

From Janine Scott

I live in New Zealand, and have two daughters. They love to read fact books that are full of fun facts and features. I hope you do, too!